♡ S. Canter ☺

Bad Day Go Away

Copyright 2014 By Sarah Canter

www.sarahcanter.com

Printed in the United States of America

Sunny Day Publishing, LLC
Akron, Ohio 44303
www.sunnydaypublishing.com
ISBN 978-0-9903823-1-7
Library of Congress Control Number: 2014953150

SUNNY DAY®
PUBLISHING, LLC
a health education company™

Dedication

Thank you to all my family and friends who have supported me during this journey! Your love and encouragement fueled this creative process.

Thank you Mom for all my treasured childhood memories of nightly bedtime stories and for instilling in me a love of reading.

Thank you to my talented and patient illustrator/visionary, Taylor Brandt, for not only making my dream come to life, but for also adding inspirational elements throughout our book!

Thank you to my former students who inspired me to write this book and helped me with the entire writing process. You have taught me more than you know!

Thank you to Mayra Porrata and the entire Sunny Day Publishing family for your guidance and help with the publishing process.

For My Readers

If you should ever have a bad day, I hope this book helps it go away! Remember, what you dream is what life brings! May your life be filled with lots of love, laughter, and an abundance of happiness!

Special Thanks

Our sincere gratitude and appreciation to Suzanne and Ralph Garrett at Tomorrow's Treasures Picture Framing & Gallery (Akron, Ohio) for photographing our artwork and also to Paul Hasson for helping us edit each page of this book!

Bad day go away!
It is not allowed
to stay!

The day is bad.
You are sad.
You want to make
yourself feel glad.

Here are things
that you can do
to help yourself
to not feel blue.

Find a place
to sit or lay.
Everything
will be OK!

4

Be very quiet.

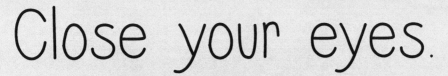

Close your eyes.

Relax your body.

Take three big sighs.

❤1 Breathe in slow...
    Breathe out slow...

❤2 Breathe in slow...
    Breathe out slow...

❤3 Breathe in slow...
    Breathe out slow...

(*Go to page 26 for more help with deep breathing.)

Breathe in deep...

Breathe out slow...

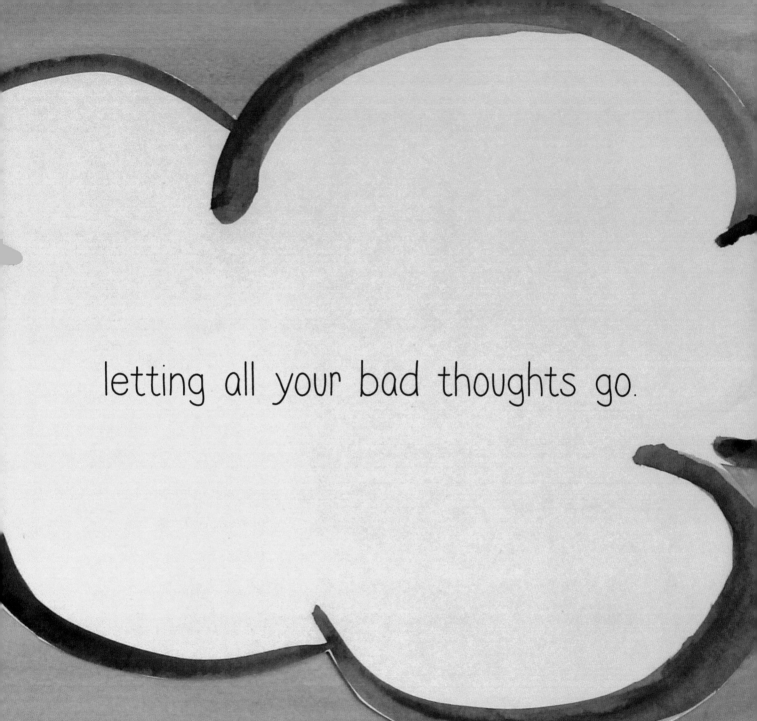

letting all your bad thoughts go.

14

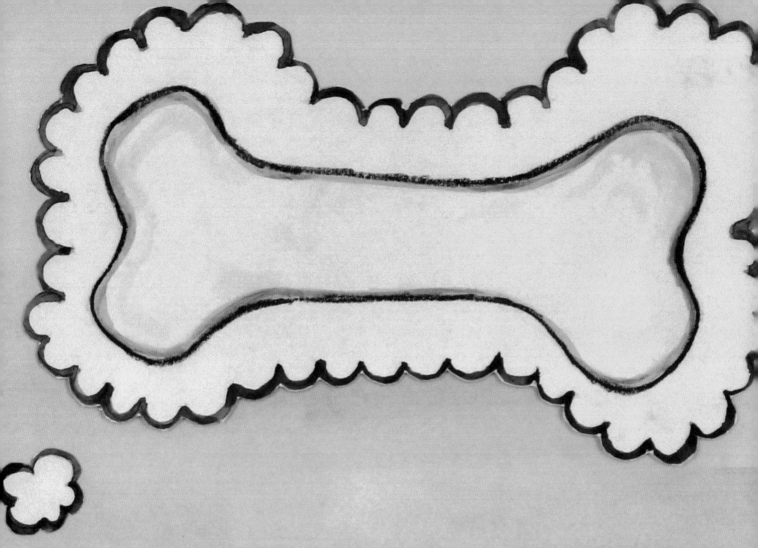

Think of only happy things!
What you dream is what life brings.

16

The bad day
starts to fade away.

It is not allowed
to stay!

Find someone you really love.
Snuggle, cuddle, get a hug.

If life does not go your way,
you can have a better day!

Time to turn the day around, flip your frown upside down!

You can feel cheerful!
Your smile will shine!
Everything will be just fine.

Your bad day has gone away!

Happiness is here to stay!

24

Ten ways to help yourself feel happier :

1. Take 3 deep breaths.

2. Stretch your body and move your body.
   Exercise can help your bad day go away!

3. Let your bad thoughts go.
   (Write down or draw a picture of the bad thoughts/feelings,
   then rip up the paper, and throw the pieces away!)

4. Talk to someone you love about your feelings.

5. Ask someone you love to give you a hug.

6. Listen to some soft music.

7. Think about your favorite things!
   You can write them down or draw them too.

8. Go outside and get some fresh air.

9. Laugh! Laughing can make you smile and feel happy!

10. Rest. Taking a short rest or nap can help you relax and feel better.

How to take 3 slow, deep breaths...

Your 1st slow, deep breath :

Breathe in slowly through your nose (or your mouth) as you count to three : 1....2...3... and fill up your tummy with air.

You can put your hand on your tummy and feel it fill up with air, as you breathe in slow !

Hold your deep breath and count to five : 1...2....3...4...5

Breathe out slowly for seven seconds : 1...2...3...4...5...6...7
Let all the air come slowly out of your mouth.

If your hand is still on your tummy, you will feel your tummy go back to normal.

Your 2nd slow, deep breath :

Breathe in slowly through your nose (or your mouth) as you count to three : 1....2...3... and fill up your tummy with air.

Hold your deep breath and count to five : 1...2...3...4...5

Breathe out slowly for seven seconds : 1...2...3...4...5...6...7
Let all the air come slowly out of your mouth.

Your 3rd slow, deep breath :

Breathe in slowly through your nose (or your mouth) as you count to three : 1....2...3... and fill up your tummy with air.

Hold your deep breath and count to five : 1...2...3...4...5

Breathe out slowly for seven seconds : 1...2...3...4...5...6...7
Let all the air come slowly out of your mouth.

*Remember, you can take deep breaths any time of the day to help you relax and feel better!
*Taking deep breaths can help your bad day go away!

The End

36523937R00020

Made in the USA
Charleston, SC
08 December 2014